Storybook Manual: An Introduction To Working With Storybooks Therapeutically And Creatively

This resource has been designed to support practitioners and parents with practical and creative ideas on how to use illustrated storybooks therapeutically with children. Whilst this book is also available to purchase as part of a set, with three therapeutic fairy tales, all the content, worksheets and activities can be used with any illustrated story. Exercises have been created to encourage imagination and free play, develop confidence and emotional literacy as well as deepen engagement and understanding of stories. It is a book that can be returned to again and again to inspire creative engagement with stories with individuals or groups.

Key features include:

- An exploration of the importance of stories to modern life, and their use as a creative and therapeutic tool
- Guidance for working with stories and their illustrations, including conversation starters, prompts and worksheets for process-orientated creative activities
- Accompanying online activities designed for specific use with the storybooks in the *Therapeutic Fairy Tales* series

This is an invaluable resource for all professionals looking to work therapeutically with stories and images. It will be particularly valuable to those working in child and family mental and emotional health, social and youth care, community and participatory arts, school and education, and specialised health and hospital environments.

Pia Jones is an author, workshop facilitator and UKCP integrative arts psychotherapist, trained at the Institute for Arts in Therapy and Education, London. At the core of her practice, Pia uses arts and story to help children and adults connect with inner resources during times of loss, transition and change. You can find out more about her work at www.silverowlartstherapy.com

Sarah Pimenta is an experienced artist, lecturer in creativity and workshop facilitator with children and adults. Her specialist art form is print-making which brings texture, colour and emotion into a variety of educational, health and community environments in the UK and abroad. You can find out more about her work at www.social-fabric.co.uk

Therapeutic Fairy Tales
Pia Jones and Sarah Pimenta
978-0-367-25108-6
This unique therapeutic book series includes a range of beautifully illustrated and sensitively written fairy tales to support children who are experiencing trauma, distress and challenging experiences, as well as a manual designed to support the therapeutic use of story.

Titles in the series include:

Storybook Manual: An Introduction To Working With Storybooks Therapeutically And Creatively
978-0-367-49117-8

The Night Crossing: A Lullaby For Children On Life's Last Journey
978-0-367-49120-8

The Island: For Children With A Parent Living With Depression
978-0-367-49198-7

The Storm: For Children Growing Through Parents' Separation
978-0-367-49196-3

Storybook Manual

AN INTRODUCTION TO WORKING WITH STORYBOOKS THERAPEUTICALLY AND CREATIVELY

Pia Jones and Sarah Pimenta

LONDON AND NEW YORK

First published 2021
by Routledge
2 Park Square, Milton Park, Abingdon, Oxon OX14 4RN

and by Routledge
52 Vanderbilt Avenue, New York, NY 10017

Routledge is an imprint of the Taylor & Francis Group, an informa business

© 2021 Pia Jones and Sarah Pimenta

The right of Pia Jones and Sarah Pimenta to be identified as authors of this work has been asserted by them in accordance with sections 77 and 78 of the Copyright, Designs and Patents Act 1988.

All rights reserved. The purchase of this copyright material confers the right on the purchasing institution to photocopy pages which bear the photocopy icon and copyright line at the bottom of the page. No other part of this publication may be reproduced, stored in a retrieval system, or transmitted in any form or by any means, electronic, mechanical, photocopying, recording or otherwise, without prior permission in writing from the publisher.

Trademark notice: Product or corporate names may be trademarks or registered trademarks, and are used only for identification and explanation without intent to infringe.

British Library Cataloguing-in-Publication Data
A catalogue record for this book is available from the British Library

Library of Congress Cataloging-in-Publication Data
Names: Jones, Pia, author. | Pimenta, Sarah, illustrator.
Title: Storybook manual : an introduction to working with storybooks therapeutically and creatively / Pia Jones and Sarah Pimenta.
Description: Abingdon, Oxon ; New York, NY : Routledge, 2020. | Series: Therapeutic fairy tales | Includes bibliographical references.
Identifiers: LCCN 2020001171 (print) | LCCN 2020001172 (ebook) | ISBN 9780367491130 (hardback) | ISBN 9780367491178 (paperback) | ISBN 9781003044628 (ebook)
Subjects: LCSH: Narrative therapy. | Metaphor--Therapeutic use.
Classification: LCC RC489.S74 J66 2020 (print) | LCC RC489.S74 (ebook) | DDC 616.89/165--dc23
LC record available at https://lccn.loc.gov/2020001171
LC ebook record available at https://lccn.loc.gov/2020001172

ISBN: 978-0-367-49117-8 (pbk)
ISBN: 978-1-003-04462-8 (ebk)

Typeset in Antitled
by Servis Filmsetting Ltd, Stockport, Cheshire

Contents

Introduction to the Storybook Manual 1

Chapter 1: Background: The ancient art of storytelling 5

- The ancient art of storytelling   6
- Using story and metaphor to make sense of the unknown and unfamiliar   7
- Fairy tales, picture books and storytelling in modern culture   9
- The bedtime story ritual   10

Chapter 2: Introduction to working with storybooks therapeutically and creatively, aims and benefits 13

- Working with storybooks therapeutically and creatively   14
- The use of storybooks to help promote therapeutic art-making   16
- Storybooks as a creative tool to explore existential challenges   17
- Storytelling and storybooks as a prompt to explore the therapeutic relationship   18

Chapter 3: Setting the scene for safe therapeutic and creative storytelling 19

- Creating the right conditions   20
- Attending to psychological processes evoked in the child and practitioner   23
- Getting ready to listen to and notice children's responses to the story   25
- Getting ready to enter the world of metaphor and speak its language   27

Chapter 4: Working with story 29

- Suggestions for conversation starters and prompts   30
- Example worksheets for process-orientated story activities   37

Contents

Chapter 5: Using stories and storybooks as a basis for creative art-making exercises..47

- Building upon the story – setting the scene for creative art-making exercises   48
- Guiding principles behind building a creative mindset   50
- Creative materials and storage of children's artwork   55
- Helping children warm up with spontaneous creative exercises   57
- An introduction to using creative art-making to explore and expand upon storybooks   59
- Top tips to remember when working with children and art-making exercises   67
- Example worksheets for process-orientated warm-up creative activities   71
- Example worksheets for process-orientated creative art-making activities   77

Summary and conclusions..87

Bibliography...89

Permissions...91

Acknowledgements

Many thanks to the Speechmark editorial and production team for all their skill in turning our Storybook Manual into a practical and creative resource. Specific thanks to Katrina Hulme-Cross, Leah Burton, Cathy Henderson and Alison Jones.

Many thanks also to Jo Parker, Tamsin Cooke and Katrina Hillkirk for their feedback and creative input into the Storybook Manual. To Eugene Hughes, who brought Sarah and I together as creative practitioners a decade ago, always supporting our work. To Louise Austin, for her scholarly insight.

A thanks goes also to Loris Malaguzzi (1920–1994) who developed the Reggio Emilia Approach which acknowledges children as authors of their own experience and puts play and experimentation at the core of children's learning. Also, to Virginia Axline (1911–1988), Donald Winnicott (1896–1971), Ann Cattanach (1937–2009) and Violet Oaklander, for inspiring us to place children's creativity and imagination at the centre of their well-being, recovery and growth.

A huge thank you to all the school children we've worked with, as well as our own children, who have strengthened our belief in the power of art to heal, connect and bring joy.

Thanks also to the storytellers and illustrators who captured our imagination either as children or adults and continue to inspire us: Eric Carle, Sandra Dieckmann, Maurice Sendak, Jackie Morris, Oliver Jeffers, Gemma O'Neill, Shaun Tan and so many others ….

Introduction to the Storybook Manual

This Manual has been designed to support practitioners with practical and creative ideas on how to use illustrated storybooks – both story and image – when working with children therapeutically. The Manual is hopefully a book that lives 'off the shelf', something that can be dipped into as and when needed.

It accompanies the *Therapeutic Fairy Tales*, a Speechmark/Routledge, Taylor & Francis series of picture books for children going through times of loss and transition, although it does not have to be used exclusively with these stories. This Manual has been created for practitioners interested in working with storybooks in general.

The Manual, after a brief historical context of oral storytelling, myth, fairy tales and metaphor, and therapeutic stories, will cover the following:

1) Creating the right conditions for working with storybooks therapeutically and creatively
2) Prompts and conversation starters on how to read and explore storybooks with children
3) Further creative ideas and exercises on how to use story and image as a therapeutic tool.

At the end of key sections, we have included worksheets with examples of process-orientated creative activities.

The Storybook Manual can be used by a range of professionals in:

- Child and family mental and emotional health
  - Talking therapists, counsellors, clinical psychologists, trainees
  - Creative therapists, art therapists, play therapists, trainees

- Social and youth care
  - Social workers, youth workers, trainees
- Schools
  - Teachers, TAs, learning support, school counsellors, SENCOs
- Community and participatory arts; theatre, performance, storytelling, art making
  - Creative arts facilitators, workshop leaders, students
- In specialised health scenarios (relevant to *The Night Crossing* in the *Therapeutic Fairy Tales* series), it may be useful for those working in hospital and hospice contexts – nurses, carers, etc.
- People who see adults in therapeutic settings and social care may find it useful to help older clients revisit themes in relation to childhood, and/or their own children.
- Although designed primarily for one-to-one work, prompts and ideas in this Storybook Manual can be adapted to group work.

It is our hope that the Manual introduces new skills based on blending creative and therapeutic fields:

1) A creative process-orientated framework for 'talking therapy' practitioners
2) A psychological process-focussed framework for creative practitioners

For the sake of clarity, throughout this Storybook Manual we refer to the therapist/social worker/responsible care-worker as the 'storyteller' or 'practitioner'. We will refer to the user as 'child' or 'client'. In exercises, we have aimed to use language that is age-appropriate for 7+ year olds. For younger children, some words and phrases may need to be adapted accordingly. Practitioners also need to be mindful that chronological and developmental age in children may not always be the same. Storybooks can also be chosen to explore particular developmental themes.

This Manual is based on the respective experiences of the authors, Pia Jones and Sarah Pimenta, in arts psychotherapy and arts education over the last 20 years. It has been formed by collecting and writing down the basics of what has worked for us. Our experiences equally draw upon the ideas and expertise of therapeutic, educational and creative thinkers dedicated to supporting children and families with emotional and creative health and well-being. Where possible, we've included sources and references.

Introduction to the Storybook Manual

It is equally our hope that the Manual not only gives guides and suggestions for practice but sparks a passion for story and creativity in all its different forms – books, theatre, animations, film, television, song – so that practitioners can inspire and be inspired by the children they work with. Equally, we hope practitioners will take this inspiration forward to encourage parents and caregivers to engage in storytelling with children. Stories are such a simple yet powerful tool to help promote bonding and building healthy relationships in families. Stories also offer children an opportunity to explore what it means to be authors of their own lives.

Chapter 1
Background: The ancient art of storytelling

Chapter 1

The ancient art of storytelling

> "Stories are the most important thing in the world.
> Without stories, we wouldn't be human beings at all."
>
> © Philip Pullman, circa 2000

Oral storytelling forms part of our collective human history. Like breathing, it appears that it's how we are made, with an innate need to share stories between families, peers and our wider communities.

Perhaps quite simply, story creates a thread for us to hang feelings and experiences, bringing a sense of order and meaning to life events. There are the stories we each tell in our daily lives, and those we inherit and receive from our wider culture. Evidence of myths, legends, folk and fairy tales are found in all corners of the world (Campbell, 1993). These ancient storytelling forms enabled generations to pass on experiences and culture to the next (Whittick, 1960). It is one of the ways that we understand and share our historical past, be that personal or collective.

In times past, storytelling often took part as a ritual, in a circle around a fire, a table, or in a special open-air place, like an amphitheatre. A designated storyteller would bring to life stories be it through their voice, physical actions, singing, music, masks and/or instruments such as a drum (Jones, 1996). This storyteller would 'guide' their audience through the story.

Our ancestors most likely told these more 'formal' stories for many reasons – to share learning with communities, to rule, to warn them, to celebrate important occasions, to preach, to explore the unknown, to entertain and enlighten.

Another important reason may have been to help people find meaning during times of painful change and loss. When going through any major life transition, unfamiliar feelings can frighten and overwhelm us, whether child or adult. Yet, attempts to block or avoid these emotions altogether can take away the very energy we need to support and guide us through times of change (Brett, 1988). Dealing with grief, loss, illness, sudden change, the vagaries of Nature, may well have fallen into the realm of story (Jung, 1984).

Using story and metaphor to make sense of the unknown and unfamiliar

As children, we learn about the world and make sense of it through story and metaphor. From an early age, objects, teddy bears and toys are imbued with real-life properties, 'as if' these objects were alive and communicating with us (Winnicott, 1971). Fairies, witches and demons, talking animals, superheroes all speak to a child's imagination. Children are naturally at ease with metaphor, speaking its language and intuiting its deeper meaning (Mills & Crowley, 1986).

Bruno Bettelheim, child psychoanalyst, proposed that reading fairy tales enabled children to explore fears and themes of growing up that perhaps felt too big and unknown to discuss openly:

> More often than not, he (the child) is unable to express these feelings in words, or he can do so only by indirection: fear of the dark, of some animal, anxiety about his body. The fairy tale takes these existential anxieties and dilemmas very seriously and addresses itself directly to them: the need to be loved and the fear that one is thought worthless; the love of life and the fear of death.
>
> (Bettleheim, 1976: 10)

Equally for an adult audience, story remains important. The struggles and adventures of 'characters' or 'heroes' in myths and stories become metaphors – imaginary vessels to carry some of the conflict and difficulty in everyday people's lives. Story enables us to bear some of life's inevitable losses by creating a safe distance between audience and material (Jennings, 1998). Yet, even when it's not our own story, if emotionally resonant, we identify with elements of a character's situation (Jones, 1996).

By wrapping existential difficulties in metaphor and symbol, story can paradoxically bring children and adults more aware of and closer to their real feelings. The Ancient Greeks (Aristotle) coined the term "catharsis" to describe what they felt happened in audiences during theatre performances; "the process of releasing, and thereby providing relief from, strong emotions" (Oxford Dictionary of Phrase and Fable, 2005).

Chapter 1

Whether feelings arrive quietly or noisily, it doesn't matter. The importance is that the experience feels real and meaningful to the audience/reader, enabling a therapeutic process to begin. As the audience projects their own feelings and experiences onto the characters, the story can be used as a tool for psychological growth.

Fairy tales, picture books and storytelling in modern culture

Like language itself, over time stories shift and change shape. Myths, fairy and folk tales have been written down, turned into poems, plays, scripts, song. Printing presses and illustration techniques have brought us beautiful picture books, tangible objects to hold, look at and share.

Pictures and images speak to different parts of ourselves (McNiff, 1992). An image can contain different elements – multi-sensory feelings, themes, conflicts, potential resolutions. Most children don't need to be taught visual literacy; they naturally respond to pictures and images in storybooks. Picture books seem designed to be shared and read together in a relational setting (Spitz, 1999). An image calls out *look at me*, as do verbal metaphors (Siegelman, 1990). This must-see quality of images enables readers to become a witness, with children often showing a real hunger to see images in picture books (Bulmer, 2000).

Stories are now told through a variety of new broadcast media; radio, film, TV, computers, tablets, mobile phones. Sharing images and photos have become an integral part of the modern world's diet. Yet, despite the speed at which technology changes, the content often doesn't. Many themes from our oldest stories still survive, finding their ways into our favourite TV programmes, songs, films and books. Just the words – *once upon a time* – evoke expectations around a storytelling experience. Traces of modern-day rituals in storytelling can be found all over the world.

Scouts/guides, forest schools, youth and drama clubs often tell stories and sing songs together. Some of these will take place in nature around a campfire. In nurseries and early school education, circle-time is a place to read out-loud stories and nursery rhymes to a group of young children. Shamans in non-Western cultures guide and heal through story and drumming. Audiences sit in groups to watch theatre and films.

Chapter 1

The bedtime story ritual

In many parts of the world, bedtime stories are another left-over of a rich oral tradition. The deceptively simple act of reading a bedtime story to a young child can be key in promoting healthy, intimate relationships. If both parties are engaged, much goes on:

1. Adult reader and child listener/s position themselves, normally in comfort, and close physical proximity, so participants can see the book, both its words and pictures.
2. As the story begins, an air of *relaxed concentration* forms. Child and adult enter another space, what is often described as a liminal or transitional space, 'another world' (Winnicott, 1971; Levine, 1992). Even the concept of time might feel different, slower, stretchy.
3. In order to bring the story to life, the reader often slows down, changing voices for different characters. The cadence of ordinary speech changes. The reader 'performs' the story, speaking the words out loud, mediating the story for the child (Spitz, 1999).
4. The child seems to gain a surprising focussing ability to spot mistakes on the part of the reader. They may say: "*You missed a bit!*"
5. For the child 'receiving' the story, they may react in different ways, soaking it up in silence, or becoming an active participant, asking questions.

6. Often, the bedtime story, offering both visual and verbal stimulus, enables children to speak more freely about their life; thoughts, feelings or worries troubling them. Making associations and links with characters in a book can help a child reflect on their own life, get in touch with their own fears and anxieties, equally encourage their problem-solving abilities.
7. The story and its pictures can serve as a container for potentially difficult and painful themes, showing children that they are not on their own (Cattanach, 1994).
8. The reader and child have been on a shared journey, often feeling close and connected, and sharing an emotional bond as a result.

Bedtime stories are important because reading stories in therapy or a therapeutic setting draw upon some of the components of the 'special' feel of bedtime stories. Bedtime stories provide clues on how to create the right conditions for working with story and image with children in a professional setting, when a safe and trusting relationship needs to be built.

Practitioners do need to be mindful that not all children will have positive associations around storytelling. If a supposed source of safety was instead a source of pain (Jennings, 2005), practitioners need to attend to any fears and difficulties communicated by children. In allowing children to voice real feelings in a safe environment, therapeutic storytelling can offer the opportunity of a reparative experience.

Chapter 2

Introduction to working with storybooks therapeutically and creatively, aims and benefits

Working with storybooks therapeutically and creatively

Working with storybooks therapeutically draws upon some of the innate power of the bedtime story ritual, and the familiarity most children will have with books and stories in some form or another. Like bedtime reading, it can be useful to think about creating a kind of theatre and performance, a special space.

However, unlike reading purely for entertainment, the aims and benefits of therapeutic storytelling are to:

- Help children connect with their own story through the medium of metaphor
- Provide a *mirror* for children's own emotions and experiences (Stern, 1995)
- Help normalise children's feelings, so they don't feel so alone in difficulty
- Validate the range of feelings and behaviours triggered in difficult situations
- Help children become aware of feelings and needs that they may be blocking
- Support children in feeling safe so they can learn to listen to their own feelings
- Help build confidence in expressing difficult emotions – giving them a language
- Activate children's imaginations to help them explore, express and make sense of thoughts, needs and feelings, some of which may be conflicting and painful
- Enable different parts of a child to come out – their own internal cast of characters

- Help children get in touch with new inner resources and qualities
- Create a greater sense of order, place and meaning during a period of chaos
- Support children in making links, thinking and reflecting about their situation
- Develop greater communication skills in general
- Help children think about the stories they are told about themselves
- Build confidence in clients to tell their own story, express, process and integrate feelings and experiences, what Bowlby (pioneer of Attachment Theory) described as *autobiographical narrative competence* (Bowlby, 1988; Holmes, 1993).

Chapter 2

The use of storybooks to help promote therapeutic art-making

A natural extension to working with storybooks is to encourage visual imagination and creative art-making with children (Winnicott, 1964). Art-making and play form the basis of children's early years education as a tool to learn and engage with the world around them. Used therapeutically, the arts are a powerful way to bring emotional landscapes to life in the outer world in a child-friendly way. Through art-making, children can start to make sense of feelings and difficult experiences, as well as invent new stories and realities.

Aims and benefits for therapeutic art and image-making

- Making images helps children externalise thoughts, feelings, experiences
- Art can hold complexity; different/conflicting emotions and non-verbal aspects
- Art images hold strong feelings in safe ways, enabling talks around self-regulation: e.g. volcanos, blowing their top or releasing steam
- The physical act of making can help release feelings for children, helping them get in touch with previously unknown, hidden emotions
- Activating imagination helps children further explore their own personal situation, empowering children as a result
- Sharing images with another is a tangible way to look and explore themes and feelings together, and can lead to children feeling witnessed and understood
- Attitudes to art-making can also flush out negative beliefs about the self, enabling practitioner and child to work on blocks to growth
- Gaining confidence in self-expression for art-making can build stronger sense of self, enabling children to become more at home with themselves, their creativity
- Image-making is another way to help children tell their own stories, helping them to make sense of or learn to stay with uncertainty
- Creative activities enable children to see their own stories from other perspectives, giving them an opportunity to see themselves differently
- Working with imagination can help activate children's problem-solving abilities
- Art-making gives permission to play with new ideas and possibilities
- Clearing up arts materials together can help children explore themes of teamwork and collaboration

Storybooks as a creative tool to explore existential challenges

Aside from exploring specific themes in the story, working therapeutically with storybooks can also serve to prompt wider discussions about the existential fears and challenges that affect everyone, child or adult, during times of loss, transition and change:

- Our relationship with feeling helpless and vulnerable
- Ideas on how and when we decide to seek and accept help
- Fears around being overwhelmed by strong, difficult emotions
- Difficulties in feeling and letting go of strong emotions
- Pacing ourselves; deciding when we don't want to go into feeling if it's too much, or not the right time
- Learning to read feelings, find a language for them, enabling better communication
- Helping us re-find a sense of centre when we feel scattered by external events
- Lessons on how we access and develop different qualities/parts of ourselves: resilience, acceptance, determination, bravery, honesty, sharing vulnerability etc
- Exploration of themes of separation and togetherness with significant others
- How we start to see ourselves and others differently during times of challenge
- Giving an opportunity to develop more compassion for self and others
- Introducing a sense of being part of a wider human family

Chapter 2

Storytelling and storybooks as a prompt to explore the therapeutic relationship

Not only can storybooks be used to explore both specific and existential themes in the life of a child, but equally they can lead to conversations about the therapy itself, exploring some of the more subtle aspects of the relationship between storyteller and child.

- Opportunities to explore feelings and themes brought up by being read to
  - Intimacy/separation
  - Control/lack of control
  - Autonomy/passivity
- What might a child be expecting in this reading context based on their past
  - Potential for being ignored/shamed/humiliated/criticised/overwhelmed, etc
  - Any neglect or abuse that a child might have experienced
- Gives children an opportunity to share real feelings and fears
- Who is leading and who is being led?
- Exploring how to set up reading in safe ways with an adult without fear of reprisal
- Reading provides opportunity to model safe rules in relationships
- Storytelling can help establish safe boundaries and mutual reward in reading

For children who have experienced neglect or abuse, having a positive storytelling experience with a safe adult can be deeply reparative.

Chapter 3
Setting the scene for safe therapeutic and creative storytelling

Chapter 3

Creating the right conditions

The right conditions needed for therapeutic and creative storytelling are the same for any therapeutic activity; the creation of a sense of safety, an open attitude, authenticity, warmth, trust, holding/containment, stillness, receptivity, an ability to listen, balancing a mental and emotional freedom with a sense of boundaries (Axline, 1947; Rogers, 1980). In addition, children benefit when practitioners bring in qualities of playfulness, acceptance, compassion and empathy (PACE model: Hughes, 2007). The aim is to create an atmosphere of *relaxed concentration*, where children are invited to participate without feeling under pressure to do so.

As storyteller, you will be a child's guide through the storybook. Before beginning, it's important to consider a child's individual needs and real-life story. The challenge is to strike a balance between not overwhelming a child while at the same time creating a safe space for feelings to emerge. Children who have experienced neglect or trauma may find entering their imagination initially difficult (Greenalgh, 1997). Working therapeutically with storybooks requires a gentle, natural pace. The process, just like feelings, cannot be rushed (Oaklander, 1988). Some key things to think about before introducing a book:

Readiness of your relationship with the child you're working with

- How long have you been working together?
  - Is there enough safety and trust?
  - Have you enough of a working alliance relationship or are you keen to use the book to help build one?
- How is this book going to fit into your existing work together?
  - Use of other storybooks

Child-led or practitioner-led

- Whose idea is it to read the book?
- Is the child asking for a story that relates to a particular theme?
- If it is the practitioner's idea, how to introduce the book in a natural way that can empower the child and help them feel their life-story is of interest and important
  - E.g. relating back to a child's reflections or questions from a previous session

- Invite the child to be a co-storyteller irrespective of who has chosen the book

Differences in chronological and developmental age in children

- As chronological and developmental age do not always correlate, it's useful to think about how old your child may be from a developmental point of view
- In some cases, older children will benefit from younger stories that deal with relevant themes to the developmental stage they are going through
- Equally, you may want to explore a particular developmental theme with a client (child or adult) and choose the story accordingly
- Or it may be a story transcends age and speaks to universal, archetypal themes

Setting up a therapeutic reading corner reflective of bedtime stories

- Explore how to create physical comfort without breaking boundaries around touch
  - Creating an opportunity to explore themes of healthy togetherness and separation/boundaries between therapist and client
  - Sitting close to a safe, responsible adult can be ultimately reparative for children who have experienced neglect or abuse, but it may also feel initially threatening
- Invite the child to create and design their own cosy reading corner or den
  - Using cushions, beanbags, blankets, depending on what's available
  - Enabling children to decide how much space they need, what feels safe
- If a child is bed-bound in hospital, with low energy levels, explore their preferences
  - Whether to listen first, to see pictures after, or do both together
  - Think about how they can experience the story in the most comfort
  - And how to make the experience feel special – for example, having torches, reading in the dark
- Having a child un-make and undo the reading corner/den can also be a way to prepare for the ending of a session

Chapter 3

Timing, pacing and delivery

- Make sure there is enough time in a session for reading and processing a story
  - You may want to stop and consider the story and pictures along the way
  - Your child may want it read again, so best not to introduce a storybook too late in a session
  - Children may also want to read parts themselves – you can invite them to do so
- When reading, try to keep a steady breathing and relaxed reading rhythm, given the natural tendency we all have to speed up
- Be aware of your tone of voice, how to make the storytelling a gentle, pleasurable auditory experience as you take the child into an imaginary world
- Try to allow the story to settle, incorporate pauses, taking cues from the child
  - Enabling digestion, listening and reflection time for you and your reader
  - So much will happen in the non-spoken, the non-verbal
- Model active listening skills where you attune to your child's needs

Explaining that this is not a school-based activity, separate from learning reading skills

- Not all children have had positive reading or learning experiences at home or school
- Based on differing skill levels and interest, the idea of storybooks may evoke positive or negative feedback in the reader, or storybooks may feel unfamiliar
- Set up therapeutic storytelling as a different or new kind of activity
  - No right or wrong, or any relation to success/failure
  - Not a test about listening and remembering the story or feedback
  - An opportunity to explore a new character's feelings, journey, story

Attending to psychological processes evoked in the child and practitioner

Remain aware of impact of storytelling process itself

Before beginning, it's useful to stay aware of the impact of the storytelling process itself on your relationship with the child; what is evoked in them and you. The very act of therapeutic storytelling, a potentially close encounter, may activate specific feelings. The child may transfer feelings from their own past experiences, either at home or at school, on the current situation. As already mentioned, in cases of neglect, abuse and trauma, the child may be activated by storytelling situations. In psychodynamic and psychoanalytic therapy, transferring the past onto the present are described in terms such as transference and countertransference, and are seen as primarily unconscious processes (Winnicott, 1947; Casement, 1985; Geldard & Geldard, 1997).

Transference is an opportunity to learn more about the child's history and inner world. It also offers an opportunity for a different, reparative experience (Balint, 1968/89). Equally, the therapist or reader will have their own countertransference responses; what is provoked in them. In order to work creatively with these dynamics, it's useful for practitioners to remain curious and aware in non-judgemental ways of what is evoked in the child. For example:

- Depending on the child's own history, working with storybooks may activate feelings around significant loss or deficits such as lack of care, attention and affection
- Stay attuned to any display of fears and/or lack of skills around reading and concentration, or any associations with failure and school
  - Notice their quality of attention, sitting back, distracted, etc ...
  - Look out for any attempts to win approval, or expectations of disapproval
  - If they disengage, it's an opportunity to learn what might be difficult
- In some cases, children may have experienced abuse such as grooming by adults through storytelling, so it's important to stay attentive to any potential triggers
- Stay aware, as therapist, of a child's need for control, merging, distraction, or sabotage, or any other acting-out behaviours that give you clues to unmet needs

Chapter 3

- One way to help empower your child is to let them lead and design a reading corner, exploring the best sitting positions, distances, what feels most safe for them
  - Establishing their role as co-storyteller
  - There may be times when they want to lead, or want you to lead, or that you find a common way together
- Storytelling can then become a reparative experience to show safe boundaries and mutual reward in reading together

Self-care for the practitioner – knowing the story and your own 'triggers'

In working with storybooks therapeutically, there is equally a need for self-care on the part of the practitioner. Given the stories that are chosen to be read may be dealing with difficult themes and feelings, as storyteller you need to know what's coming. Being aware of how the story affects you personally will help separate out your own feelings from potential countertransference moments that may emerge in the session with your child/reader.

- Reading the story in advance will flag up emotional areas where you might feel activated, enabling you to work through feelings beforehand in preparation
- Practise and rehearse it out-loud beforehand so you get a feel for the material
- Equally, it's worth thinking about your own bedtime story experiences, or associations around school reading, whether these were positive or difficult experiences
  - How will you respond if a child corrects/criticises you?
  - Or doesn't seem to be listening?
- Being able to laugh gently at yourself around reading skills might help you connect with your child and move reading away from school associations of getting it right or wrong, instead modelling skills such as flexibility, resilience and permission to make mistakes
  - Did I say that word differently to how it's written?
  - Yes, I've always found that word tricky, it's like a tongue-twister …
  - How about you … what words do you find tricky?

Getting ready to listen to and notice children's responses to the story

A key benefit of working with storybooks therapeutically is to provide an opportunity to explore their relevance to the child's inner world. A few things to keep an eye out for:

- Notice non-verbal responses: a child's body posture, breathing, sighs, colouring in cheeks, movement, restlessness, stillness, silence all communicate responses to a story. Different children will have their own preferences in exploring a story
  - You may want to pause, take your time after each page, to discuss
  - You and your child may want to sit in silence after the story to let feelings emerge naturally or your child may speak spontaneously and take the lead
  - Or equally, there may be moments when you want to prompt discussion
  - Perhaps your child is withdrawing or not engaging, showing you that the story, or a part of it, feels too much at this time
- Try to make reading a shared and collaborative journey where you are both going on a voyage of discovery, rather than setting yourself up as expert reader/ teacher/therapist. Where relevant and appropriate, you might want to take turns and share the reading together
  - Starting suggestions with phrases such as "let's look at this together", "let's read this together", help build a sense of co-creation
  - Make sure the child knows they have a role as co-storyteller if they want it
  - Introduce the story as a starting point for both of your questions and conversation, rather than setting it up as the way things are or should be
- It's natural for children and adults to express personal tastes. However, rather than taking any 'this is good or bad' comment at face value, follow up by exploring the meaning behind these statements. Here lies an opportunity to move away from absolutes – either/or statements – and explore what it's like to see different elements side by side
  - What is it that you really like/don't like about this character, this bit?
  - What is it that feels a bit difficult, or that seems to interest you here?

Chapter 3

- I notice you are really drawn to this page/I notice you turned the page quickly
- What's it like to see this character you don't like next to the one you do?
- How do each of them feel being next to each other?
- If you'd like to move them apart, where would you move them, how far?

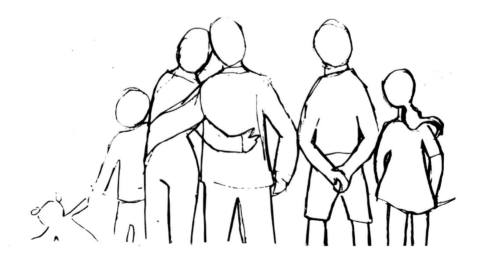

Getting ready to enter the world of metaphor and speak its language

Metaphor creates its own world within a story, outside of the rational and the logical. Rather like the dreams we have while sleeping, metaphor responds well to its own language (McNiff, 1992). Staying in metaphor and the make-believe can help build a sense of trust and safety in children, rather than too direct communication which can feel intrusive or overwhelming. Sometimes, adults are tempted into making premature links with the real, outer world, which can interrupt a child's own imaginative process. At the beginning, we'd recommend staying inside the world of metaphor and imagination with your child (Oaklander, 1988). Below are a few pointers to help facilitate the imaginative process.

- Model curiosity about characters, creatures, habitats in the stories you're reading
- From the outset, stay attuned to notice the visual and verbal metaphors that speak most strongly to the children – it could be the habitat in the books or the characters themselves, or other creatures. Follow a child's natural interest and focus. It might be something completely unexpected and different to your own preconceptions
  - Where possible, don't make assumptions of what a metaphor means and wait for a child's description before offering up your own
    - This scary monster in your eyes might not be wholly so for a child
    - Or equally a friendly character might raise questions for a child
  - Look together at where they live, and what the characters are doing – are they hiding, jumping out, or conflicted, torn in two?
- Try to stay attuned to the qualities and literal function of the metaphors that a child focusses on; be it a cloud, an animal, an island, a doorway, an obstacle. This offers up opportunities to explore polar themes and what might lie between – for example:
  - If it's a gate, you can explore themes of open and shut, or half-shut
  - If it's an island, explore themes of safety and isolation, and bridges
- Role-play and dialogue are simple techniques which can bring any metaphoric element of a story to life for children. For example:
  - If this creature or magic object could speak, what might it say or do?
  - "Let's make-up a conversation between two characters or objects"

- Metaphor can also be used to invite reflection on the therapeutic process together
  - If a child is finding it hard to end a session, you can use the story metaphor itself, for example: "it looks like we're both finding it hard to leave this Island, Cave, Mountain, etc ..."
  - "This character has gone off and hidden ... I wonder if that's what you'd like to do here sometimes too?"
- Stay attuned to whether your child wants to stay within the story and metaphor framework or if they prefer to make links to their own real-life situation. Ideally, it's better not to guide them out unless they start making personal references to their own story
- When/if they are ready, children may start making links to other stories, or friends, or family members. At the right time, linking can be a useful tool in creating layers of additional meaning and context, also empowering a child to make their own insights. It's a joy to see a child surprise themselves by making their own meaning, rather than have it given to them by an adult. Yet, we need to be careful here. Some children may not want to 'own' particular aspects of a story. In some cases, being too direct about similarities can close off further exploration. The story itself may be enough to resonate with a child's themes (Oaklander, 1988; Jennings, 1998).

Chapter 4
Working with story

Chapter 4

Suggestions for conversation starters and prompts

In the sections that follow, we've outlined a variety of prompts to help children engage and reflect on themes when working with storybooks. Given the wide range of conversation starters included here, it would certainly be counterproductive and intrusive to use them all. Any therapeutic interventions – questions, suggestions, observations, role-play activities, creative exercises – need to be selected and rotated in ways that feel natural in the room. Too much questioning can lead to a child withdrawing and/or waiting for you to do the work. The idea is to build a sense of wonder and curiosity about storybooks.

Where possible, listen to the child first and frame any reflections or questions using a child's own language. At other times, it may be that sitting in silence together is most appropriate. In revisiting the book, it could be that some sections become more relevant. Taking your lead from the children will help determine which therapeutic intervention is most needed, and equally, tell you when it's time to take a break and/or stop. It can be useful to think of any therapeutic intervention as an invitation – a key to open your child's story.

Immediate responses after reading the story for the first time

- I wonder what is happening in this story, what's going on?
- Anything that stays with you, stands out? Any surprises?
  - If needs be, the practitioner can model their own response, "for me, I was drawn to this bit here …" or "I didn't expect this to happen … how about you?"
- Can you show me any pictures that grab your attention, make you curious?
  - Ones you like, or ones you find difficult and/or really touch you?
- I notice that you really wanted to stay a bit longer on these pages
- If beneficial, invite children to put their finger on a particular image of interest
  - Let's look at this together
  - What does this image make you feel/think of?
  - What is it about this image that attracts you?
  - If this page were to come to life, what might we see happen?
- I wonder what this story leaves you with overall – feelings, thoughts, questions

Working with story

After a first reading, sometimes it's nice just to take time to go through all the pictures again

- Let's look together at all the pictures again slowly – e.g. Look at this!
- What do you notice is going on in each image?
- What elements draw you in, make you curious?
- Discuss together which page/s are your favourite
- Anything new surprises, going through the book again?

Entering the character's world, exploring their feelings

- Let's look at the characters and what happens to them during this story
  - What do they want or wish for?
- How do they deal with or respond to changes in their lives?
- When do they show their real feelings, and when do they hide them?
- Let's look at what the character is feeling in different pictures
  - Explore facial expressions, body postures together
  - Is there more than one feeling? (Conflicting feelings, or changes over time)
  - The practitioner can lead this: "I notice here, she feels this, then it changes"
- Let's look at what's hard or challenging for the characters
  - Events, experiences, decisions, feelings, dilemmas
- Let's look at what's supportive, comforting and/or freeing for the characters
  - Events, experiences, decisions, feelings, resolutions
- Can you imagine what it would be like to be this character?
  - What might you be feeling in their place?
  - Is there anything different that you would want to do in their place?
- Which character would you most like to be in this story?
- Let's act out different scenes together from the story
  - How does it feel to step into these characters' shoes?
  - I wonder what everything looks like from this point of view

Relationships/friendships between key characters

- What do you see happening between the main characters in the story?
  - How would you describe what goes on?
- What might be difficult or challenging between them?

Chapter 4

- What do you imagine they are trying to change or make happen?
  - What's important to them, what are their interests?
- What do you see that works well and not so well between characters?
- What might characters need to say or tell each other that they are keeping to themselves at the moment?
- What do you think their lives might have been like before this story?
  - Any sense of back-story, or prequel, that might have led up to this point?
- What else do you think needs to happen between characters in the story?

Exploration of transition, loss and change

- What do the main characters learn in the story about themselves, and others?
- How do they change through the story, and/or what changes for them?
- What kind of personal qualities do these characters develop in the story?
  - Help children find their own language for qualities such as acceptance, resilience, bravery, vulnerability, independence, sadness, relief etc …
- How do the pictures show that these characters change and grow?
  - Which pictures show this?
- Moments of a dilemma or decision-making
  - What do you think makes this character decide or behave the way they do?
- Let's look to see if any pictures feel particularly supportive of change
  - Do any communicate a sense of comfort/peace/hope/safety?

Obstacles and blocks on the character's path

- What or who gets in the way of the character's story?
- What kind of obstacles do they have to deal with?
- How do they get around obstacles and difficulties?
- What new skills do they have to learn to get around obstacles?
- What other obstacles might they meet on their journey?

Engaging with ideas of asking for help and self-support

- What or who helps the main characters in the story?
  - What are they like these 'helpers'?
  - What qualities do they have?

- How do they help the main characters, what's useful?
  - I wonder what it is they do or say that gives hope/comfort/understanding?
- What's it like for the characters to ask for or accept help in these stories?
  - What are some of the challenges to asking for help?
- How do the characters help and support themselves through the story?
  - Explore qualities, strengths and anything they might find hard
- What kind of creature/character would you invent to help children?
  - Let's make up a story about your creature/character

Validation of feelings of characters in a story

Storybooks offer an opportunity to model empathy, understanding and compassion for characters, their feelings and motivations, validating what they are going through. Some useful phrases can be:

- I imagine that must be so hard for that character
  - In this situation, feeling this, and also feeling that
- I can see why that character might cry, hide, shake or shout here
- That decision must be difficult to make, I wonder what helped them make it?
- What a lot of courage (or other quality) that character shows by being/doing x, y, z
- Invite the child to make their own commentary and observations
  - Make links to storybooks or films they know, if relevant
- It's an opportunity to notice qualities the child has shown while working with you

Exploring and using habitats as a metaphor

- Let's look at what the pictures show us about where the characters live
- Can you imagine what it would be like to live here? The weather, landscape, etc ...
- Use any place of the story as a metaphor – islands, bridges, home, etc
  - E.g. What it would it feel like to be on an island, how do we get off islands, what's it like to get stuck on an island?
- I wonder if where the characters live change through the story?
- How would you improve where these characters live? What do you think they need?

Chapter 4

Parts of the story that don't make sense or invite us to question

- Can you show me any parts or pictures in the story that don't make sense to you?
- Is there anything the characters do or say that leave you with questions?
- What would you do here instead? Would you do or say something different?
  - Would you get the characters to behave differently?

Exploring choices and decision-making

- Sometimes characters in books must make difficult decisions and/or actions
  - What do you think it's like for them to make these?
  - Why do you think they chose what they did?
  - What might you do in their situation?
- What if they were to make a different choice or decision?
- Experiment with inventing a new story based on a different choice or decision

Imagining alternative outcomes/endings

- What do you think might happen next, after the end of this story?
- If you were going to change or retell any part of the story, what would it be?
- Use role-play to retell the story
  - What would you have these characters do, if it were up to you?
  - What helpers would you send them and how would they help?
- What qualities and strengths would you give your characters?
  - What might they look like? How might they be different?
- Is there anything you feel that is left unsaid in the book or doesn't make sense?

Exploring the story through the eyes of a different character

- I wonder if there is another character you are interested in?
  - It might be another main character or someone/something in the background
- What might this story be like from their point of view?
- Step in their shoes, paws, being, etc. – what would they see, hear, experience?
- What might be difficult or comforting/reassuring for them?
- What are they learning through this story?

Working with story

- If you could tell the story through another character, who would it be, what would their story be?
- Bring to life through role-play and acting out scenes

Taking a break in the storytelling

If a child initiates a break, respect their wishes, and follow up in a gentle, curious manner:

- I notice we've left the story here, maybe there is something difficult in this story?
- I wonder if there is something else that's taken your interest?
  - Can you tell me/show me?
- Look out for any links to the story or feelings in the story in the activity that the child might be now choosing
- Explain to the child that it's up to them if they want to go back to the book

Looking at endings

- Many stories give us happy endings, but often life doesn't turn out like that
  - There are different endings and sometimes new, unexpected beginnings
- Explore in the stories what kinds of endings come up for characters
  - How do they deal with what happens to them?
  - What do they imagine happening afterwards?
  - I wonder what kind of new beginnings happen (if relevant/appropriate)?
- Let's look at what feelings come up when dealing with endings
  - Sadness, anger, other strong feelings – it's natural to feel these
- What/who can help us with our feelings around endings?

Making links with children's real-life stories and feelings

If a child makes links to their own experiences, stay with their natural focus of interest:

- You said that you sometimes feel the same way, can you say a bit more?
  - Have you ever had something happen like this to you?
  - What's it been like for you? What have you found difficult, or helpful?
  - In what ways has your experience been different?

Chapter 4

- What has been your experience around help?
  - What and who is helping you?
  - Anyone you'd like to help you?
  - Any questions you wish you could ask?
- Can you share something about your own feelings?
  - Where you feel fear or worry in your body?
  - Or hope, calm and comfort?
  - What helps calm you down, what helps make you feel safe?
- Help children see how qualities like bravery, compassion develop over time
  - Not necessarily innate or fixed, 'made not born' through experiences
  - Help children locate specific qualities in themselves and others
  - I wonder what you are learning, about yourself, and others?

Making links with other stories from different media

- I wonder if these pictures/images remind you of anything else you've seen?
  - Other stories, pictures, comics, films, games, etc
- What are some of your favourite stories, characters?
- Any stories you've read again and again, or films you've seen many times?
- What is it about these stories and characters that interests you?
- What are their challenges? What do they learn? How do they change?
- Any images, pictures or lines that you find supportive?
- If you could create your own library of support?
  - Make a list of films, books, cartoons, etc, to be included here

In reading and discussing storybooks in reflective ways, children are invited to connect with and express feelings around their own story. In this way, the storybooks can serve as tools for psychological release, understanding and growth.

EXAMPLE WORKSHEETS
Worksheets for process-orientated story activities

Chapter 4: Example worksheets

Worksheet for process-orientated story activities

CREATE A NEW STORY FROM ONE STORYBOOK PICTURE

Aim: To activate children's imaginations and engage them in creative storytelling

Creative medium: Role-play and dramatic enactment

STEPS and INSTRUCTIONS

Choose one picture from your storybook as a start-point
- Something that interests you and makes you curious, even if you don't know why
- It might be a character, their actions, or a colour, a shape, another creature, a detail

Look at what's going on in the page
- Have a good look from different angles, turning the page upside down
- Imagine that you are looking under a microscope at this picture
  - The special machine that makes things that are small look bigger
- Or equally, imagine that you zoom out, and look at this page from far away
- What do you notice and see, the more you look?
  - Colours, details, anything else?

Imagine that somehow magically, this page comes to life
- What do you imagine we'd see, hear, notice from this page?
- How do the characters move, speak?
- What happens next?

Make up your own story starting with Once Upon a Time ...
- I'd like to invite you to tell your own story about this page coming to life
- To give your story a beginning, a middle and an ending
- Can you tell me your story?

Reflection and discussion
- Discuss together your new story – what's it like to make up a new one?
- What's different from the other story, what's similar?

Worksheet for process-orientated story activities

TELLING A STORY THROUGH THE EYES OF A DIFFERENT CHARACTER

(E.g. imagine what the Cinderella story looks like from the Ugly Sisters' point of view)

Aim: To activate children's imaginations and engage them in storytelling, exploring what it's like to see a story from different points of view, promoting empathy and understanding

Creative medium: Role-play and dramatic enactment (can be expanded to other creative media such as puppets, objects, drawing and painting arts materials)

STEPS and INSTRUCTIONS

Choosing a storybook and a different character that you'd like to focus on
- In storybooks, we often see a story through the eyes of one character
- Let's look together at other characters in this story
  - A creature/person/object, whatever you'd like
- Let's choose one of these other characters to explore
  - It might be one that is behaving in a different way from the main character
  - Or one that is behaving very badly
  - Or simply someone/something you are curious about

Let's step into this character's eyes, feet/paws, point of view
- Let's get to know this new character – what's it like to be them?
- What does the world look like to them?
- What are they feeling, thinking, seeing?

Let's re-imagine and tell the story from this new character's point of view
- Starting the story with Once Upon a Time ... tell their story, a start, middle and end
- How are they seeing the story and what happens to them?
- What kind of new ending might they be looking for?

Chapter 4: Example worksheets

Reflection and discussion
- Exploring the wishes, needs, difficulties of this character
- What's making them behave in the way they do?
- What might they be looking for?

Worksheet for process-orientated story activities

INVENTING A MAGIC HELPER FOR CHILDREN

(Like the fairy godmother or a talking animal in fairy tales)

Aim: To activate children's imaginations and engage them in storytelling, enabling them to get in touch with inner resources and self-support

Creative medium: Role-play and dramatic enactment (can be expanded to other creative media such as drawing, painting, clay, puppet-making, depending on resources)

STEPS and INSTRUCTIONS

Creating a Magic Helper
- In storybooks, we often see helpers that support characters through their journeys
- I'm going to invite you to make your own Magic Helper
- It can be a creature/animal/person/object, whatever you'd like

Let's find out about this Magic Helper
- What does it look/sound/behave like?
- Where does it live, and what is its name?
- What kind of children does it want to help?

Chapter 4: Example worksheets

Calling the Magic Helper
- How do we get the Magic Helper to come?
- What is this Magic Helper's special power or gift?
- How can this Magic Helper help?

Let's tell a story about the Magic Helper
- Starting with Once Upon a Time ... there was a child who needed some help ...
- Tell a story about a child who asks for help
- How does the child call the Magic Helper?
- How does the Magic Helper arrive, and how do they help the child?

Reflection and discussion of the Magic Helper
- Exploring the gifts of the Magic Helper
- What does it leave the children it helps?
- How do we find ways to help ourselves, help others?

Worksheet for process-orientated story activities

CREATING CHARACTERS TO REPRESENT DIFFERENT FEELINGS

Aim: To activate children's imaginations and engage them in storytelling, helping them to explore different feelings and how these might sit alongside each other

Creative medium: Role-play and dramatic enactment (can be expanded to other creative media such as drawing – cartoon characters/Manga characters, painting, clay, puppet-making, depending on resources)

STEPS and INSTRUCTIONS

Exploring feelings – choosing one that feels good, and one that doesn't feel so good
- What are all the different feelings we can have – good and not so good
  - Could be anger, sadness, shyness, confidence, embarrassment, etc …
- Now let's choose two feelings, one that feels good, one that feels difficult
- Let's think about what these two might feel like inside our bodies
- Where in our bodies/how do we feel them?

Inventing characters for these two different feelings
- I wonder what these feelings might look like if we brought them to life as characters?
  - Animals, vegetables, objects, anything you like
- What would they look/sound/behave like?
- Where might they live, and what would their names be?
  - Can think about alliteration – Angry Angus, Confident Carl
- Encourage children to play with funny names

Let's bring them to life by acting how they would be
- How does each move and talk?
- What would their catch phrase be?
- Act them out

Putting them side by side
- How do they feel about each other?
- What might they say or do? How might they talk to each other?
- What does the world look like from their point of view?

Reflection and discussion
- What's it like for these two feelings to exist side by side?
- How can we help them listen to each other?
- What do they each need?

Worksheet for process-orientated story activities

RETELLING AND MAKING UP YOUR OWN STORY
Changing a big choice that a character makes

Aim: To activate children's imaginations and engage them in creative storytelling, to explore themes of decision-making, cause and effect, and responsibility

Creative medium: Role-play and dramatic enactment (to be extended to other creative media if available)

STEPS and INSTRUCTIONS

Let's start with a storybook and find a page when the character makes an important choice
- Now, we are going to change the choice this character makes in this story
- You have the power to change the story
- What does this character decide to do instead?

Look at how this new choice changes the story
- What happens next in the story?
- What new obstacles might happen to your character?
- What new ending happens?

Let's retell this new story, starting with Once Upon a Time ...
- What happens to all the characters?
- You can encourage the child to use objects in the room as characters

Reflection and discussion
- Discuss together your new story
- What's changed for the characters now?
- Think about how the choices we make change what happens in our own lives

Chapter 5
Using stories and storybooks as a basis for creative art-making exercises

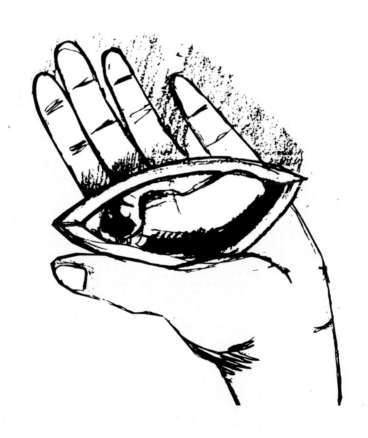

Building upon the story – setting the scene for creative art-making exercises

As well as prompting conversations, working therapeutically with storybooks provides other creative opportunities to support children. A natural extension to exploring story metaphors is to invite children to respond by inventing their own. Bringing inner worlds to life through visual imagination, play and creative art-making can be an empowering experience for children. There is something deeply holding when personal feelings, thoughts and experiences are externalised through creative arts media and witnessed by another. Creative art-making can be another way to explore difficult life themes indirectly, without putting children under too much pressure or scrutiny (Geldard & Geldard, 1997).

Working with art needs to be adapted to meet the natural energy levels of children. If working with chronically or terminally ill children, exercises need to be adapted to minimise effort. Instead of physical activity, images can be explored mentally and gently though the imagination. Less is more, as many interventions may not be appropriate. On the other hand, when working with children who find it hard to sit still or with high levels of energy, the practitioner will need to adapt exercises to help bring a sense of grounding and containment. It's important to be mindful of your child's context when introducing creative exercises.

Another consideration is working with a child's sense of judgement (and sometimes the practitioner's) around the finished art product. Unfortunately, the way art is taught in most schools is still based mainly on technique and skill. It can take time for both practitioner and child to shift into a freer way of art-making that is based on self-expression, process and exploration with the materials rather than strong attachments to product or results.

In a similar way to how transference was mentioned in Chapter 2, children and practitioners can transfer their own past experiences from art in the classroom on to therapeutic art-making. Some adults can feel uncomfortable and or fearful about introducing creativity exercises. However, when children voice "I can't make, draw, do this", it can be a valuable inroad into exploring negative self-beliefs and attitudes, and their needs for reassurance.

If a creative mindset can be built together, there can be some very real, tangible rewards for the child in terms of new skills – a stronger capacity for reflection, curiosity, honesty, flexibility, resilience, playfulness, an ability to see things from different points of view and more confidence in their creativity.

Chapter 5

Guiding principles behind building a creative mindset

In order to help move a child into the role of 'art-maker/creator/author', a few basic principles are explained below. Some may seem obvious, yet if forgotten or neglected, they will impact the creative art-making process. Practitioners are aiming to build a safe space for natural creativity and art-making to emerge.

Checking in with own relationship to creativity as practitioners

Before initiating creative activities with children, it can be useful for practitioners to check in with their own relationship to working with art and how comfortable they feel around using their imagination. Children will look to the practitioner to model a creative mindset.

Whereas some practitioners may have negative memories of school and reading/academic work, others can feel uncomfortable when moving into the realm of art-making. Arts facilitators will also have their own schooling (and potentially unrealised dreams) about their own art. In order not to let personal attitudes get in the way of natural art therapy processes, it can be useful to flush out thoughts and associations to art.

Using storybooks for creative art-making exercises

A few questions for the practitioner that we'd suggest scribbling down answers and/or making your own image as exploration

- What do the words 'art', 'imagination', 'creativity' and 'play' evoke in you?
- How was creativity and playing treated in your family? At your school?
- What were your experiences of making art as a child?
  - Positive or negative? What made them so?
- What are some of your beliefs about artists and creative people?
  - (Even if you are one, this can be useful)
- What hidden wounds might you have around creativity?
- What immediate associations do you have of art therapy?
- What do you believe art therapy can do, and can't do?
- Take a blank page, and put down anything, words, images that capture some of this

Being aware of potential blocks, which may tap into those of the child you're working with, can help practitioners stay grounded in the case of negative responses from children. The idea is not to deny these but to find ways to learn from them. Below are some ways to introduce art-making that encourage a creative and less judgemental attitude from the beginning.

Taking time to explain that this is a different kind of art-making from school

- Here, art is going to be used as another language to explore parts of ourselves
- Establish different 'rules' that you will be working with in this context
  - Not about making pretty or beautiful art to hang up on walls
  - No right or wrong, not a test, but about exploration and staying curious
  - Using art to bring outside what's inside us, to share with another
  - Using art to explore things from a different point of view
  - Any 'mistakes' are welcome here – they are a tool for learning
- Can write out 'rules' from school around art-making, then throw in the bin

Use collaborative and friendly language throughout, focussing on process not product

- "Let's have a go," or "let's see what happens," or "let's do it together" can help build a collaborative and friendly atmosphere with children

Chapter 5

- Help children practise getting in touch with mental images, before making anything, so they can become more confident in using their imaginations
  - Using phrases such as – "can you see anything in your mind/does anything come to mind, do you picture anything in your head as I say that?"
  - Sometimes asking a child to describe something first can help before asking them to show you anything on paper
- Resist the temptation (however hard) to compliment any creations made so that you don't collude with a child's wish to please you
  - Instead of saying "that's so good", keep observations focused on the process
  - E.g. "look at that, I'm curious, I notice, that's interesting, can you tell me ...";
    "I can see how much effort that's taken you," or "look at these colours you've used here" or "what a lot of energy there is"
  - Try to move away from judgements "I like/I don't like" or "good/bad"
  - Sometimes it's useful to reflect on a child's need for approval – "It sounds like you are looking for someone to tell you how well you're doing ..."

Working with client's negative responses to creative exercises

Whereas much is admirable in the growth mindset so often practised in schools and workplaces, too much focus on positivity can sometimes get in the way of therapeutic work:

- Try to welcome any ambivalence or refusal by children regarding art-making
- Any reasons voiced, "I can't, I'm not good, this is rubbish," are an opportunity to model compassion and empathy around difficult feelings being voiced
  - "I'm so glad you told me this, I can imagine it might be quite hard to say"
  - Giving permission for the negative to exist without trying to make it positive
- Avoid reassurance (hard as it can be) and use any negativity as a tool to learn more
  - What experiences might you have had that makes you think this?
  - What feelings come with this? What's it like to say this here?
  - That sounds difficult, is there anything you're worried about here?
- Blocks and resistance are a normal and healthy part of the therapeutic process
  - Which often includes a very valid need by children to test the therapist/ practitioner
  - Working with this enables more trust to be built in the relationship

- Normalising difficulty helps, as do phrases; "we're going to give this a go," or "let's see how this turns out," but it's also important to show you can sit with a child's fears
  - It also helps children with perfectionist traits understand that sometimes we need to practise and get used to something rather than just immediately know how to do it straightaway
- Often children's artwork will have more flow as they go through the therapy reflecting their own inner journey

Practitioner's role as witness

- When starting out, it can feel uncomfortable to sit and watch a child make art as an observer, yet the act of witnessing art-making is crucial to supporting a creative process
  - How to 'be' in the room and give attention to your client and their artwork
  - Balance between being encouraging and letting a child take the initiative
- As practitioner, it might be useful to think about your own experiences of being witnessed – what supported you, made you feel comfortable?
  - If not childhood experiences, then experiences during training
  - Any examples of what didn't feel supportive – what makes the difference?
- Be ready to respond with curiosity to any negative feedback from a child
  - A child may feel you are watching or judging them and their efforts
  - Can be an opportunity to explore the therapeutic relationship – what children think you are looking for, what they are being asked to do
  - An opportunity to explore how a child is experiencing you, and to re-state how therapy has a different role to school or home

Practitioner's role as creative collaborator

- Equally, there may be times when it is useful to join the child in creative activity
  - Acting out pieces of the story, creating new dialogues and roles
- Having someone make alongside can be reparative for children who have experienced little input in this area, and help them build confidence in their creativity
- When responding to a child's invitation to participate, try to stay mindful of what may be behind their request and what need they are looking to be answered

Chapter 5

Not being afraid of pauses and silence – using them as a starting point for creativity

- Modern life has become filled with technological devices, so some children (and adults) might not be used to having silence and down-time without background stimulation
- Yet creativity often arises from silence, which can appear as 'empty' or 'dead' moments
  - It can take time to learn to sit with silence and use it for growth
  - Differentiate your own discomfort as practitioner from that of a child
  - Making sure there's time for 'being' and not always 'doing' and 'busyness'
- Don't assume what silence from a child means
  - Silence can mean many different things for a child
  - Sitting with silence without rushing for answers (within reason) can sometimes also be a holding experience and give a child thinking time

Encouraging a slower pace – less is so often more

- School days are often tightly structured, packed with activities, and children are used to having their time filled
- Where possible, try to move away from a sense of productivity and doing a lot
  - Cultivating listening and *relaxed concentration* instead of filling up time
- Be mindful of not rushing sessions, allowing plenty of room/time around creative activities for discussion and reflection
- A slower pace for sessions can feel strange at first to children (and adults) yet it's an opportunity to give thoughts, feelings and creativity much needed time and space
- Pacing sessions can help model the same rhythm to children and also help minimise the risk of children feeling overwhelmed

Creative materials and storage of children's artwork

Not all environments have dedicated space to store specialist arts materials. Here are a few ideas for items that can help inspire children's creative responses and expressive mark-making.

First off, one creative medium that doesn't take any storage space is role-play – the use of dialogue and dramatic enactment. All you need is an ability to play with your imagination.

- Through role-play, voice and physical actions, children can be invited to bring stories and characters to life. They can also create new dialogues between characters

In addition to role-play, we've listed creative materials below that can be scaled up or down, depending on the space available.

- An easy start-point is pencil and paper, which is familiar and simple
- From here, a child can expand and use colour – coloured pencils, crayons, pastels, chalk and oil pastels, felt-tips, paint, coloured paper and tissue
- Different coloured papers can be effective – chalk pastels on dark backgrounds jump out, and children often enjoy experimenting and smudging colours
- Papers and cardboard are great because you can use recycled paper/card – wrapping papers, old parcels with bubble wrap, shoeboxes, cupcake cases, be as inventive as you like
- Tissues and papers can be easily torn and sculptured. With scissors and glue, you can experiment with layering and collage
- Fabrics can also be very effective – they can be used to explore patterns or wrap/unwrap and hide/reveal objects. Wool, balls of felt, buttons, combined with fabrics can be used to make puppets and creatures
- Natural objects – stones, pebbles, sand, shells – can also be very effective, connecting children with a sense of Nature
- Some early years toys, such as a Slinky or a Hoberman sphere (expanding ball), which children can animate, choosing how and where to move them in a space
- A collection of postcards can be useful as small ready-made images that children can pick and choose between
- Balloons can be useful in aiding breathing exercises and creative games

Chapter 5

Other more specific creative materials, if there is space to store them safely, include:

- Sand tray with a selection of small objects – figurines, objects, toy cars
- Plastic or paper masks
- Clay or Play-Doh (or equivalents) for easy moulding and sculpting
- Puppets – animals can be fantastic – a turtle, a monkey for representing different ways of being, also fairy tale characters can help expand on storybook work
- Dressing up box, hats, scarves, etc, where children can play different roles

Safe storage of children's creative work

One element of storage that cannot be compromised is looking after children's own artwork. Sometimes this can be difficult in organisations because space is nearly always at a premium. However, keeping children's creations safe is vital to building trust between child and practitioner. Safe storage also communicates an important sense of containment of the therapeutic and creative process by the larger environment. A cupboard that can be locked is a useful start.

In terms of storage to protect creative work, boxes around the size of shoeboxes can be useful ways to store children's smaller pieces of artwork whereas large A3 or A2 folders with handles can store larger items. These kinds of creative containers can help children really value what they make in sessions. Children can be invited to decorate boxes to make it their own, as well as name their folders. Ideally, for longer term work, try to encourage children to keep their creative work in their folders and/or boxes during sessions. Creative work can then be reviewed at the end of therapy and taken home.

Helping children warm up with spontaneous creative exercises

Below is a list of creative activities to help work with images around storybooks, starting with warm-ups, before leading on to other more story-related exercises. As in the last chapter on story, a range of ideas have been suggested so that practitioners can pick and choose. As before, it would be counterproductive to use too many. Less is more and, wherever possible, it's best to follow children's interest.

Basic shared warm-up creative exercises can help encourage familiarisation with creative materials, as well as help model a creative freedom around therapeutic art-making which is different from technical school-based activities. They also help build confidence for later exercises.

Examples of warm-up starter exercises

- Let's make marks on the paper, in tune with our breathing
  - Encourage slowing down, or other speeds, slower, faster
  - What shapes and patterns have we made, without realising?
- Scribble game – let's both make a scribble in 2 seconds and swap
  - Let's look together at what or who is hiding in our scribbles
  - Who/what have you found?
  - Invite children to swap from their usual writing hand to non-writing hand
- How about picking up a crayon, let it take/lead your hand around the paper?
  - Or equally, follow your hand, let it take/lead the crayon around the paper
  - Experiment with directing the pen – how does a crayon walk, swim, fly, crawl?
- Doodle on paper together, look at the images that 'appear' in the doodles
  - Colour these in, make up imaginary characters, figures, habitats
- Finger-drawing – draw invisible shapes with your fingers before picking up a crayon to draw them
- Invite the child to draw round hands, and colour in/decorate any way they wish
  - Explore the different ways we use our hands
  - Discuss what the child might like to do/make in this creative space
- Colour mood collages
  - Choose colours that make you feel different emotions – happy/sad/angry
  - Make an abstract collage using torn edges or cut edges of coloured paper

Chapter 5

- Music mood collages
  - Let's play some mood music and close our eyes
  - Listening to music, let's make marks in response to what we are hearing
  - Can be useful to compare and show how each person had different response
  - Can also explore with different kinds of art materials

How children find these warm-up activities can help you explore the experience of art-making and any challenges that might arise.

- Talk together about what you both noticed through doing these creative activities
  - How did you find doing/making this?
  - What is it like to make this kind of free art and not worry what it looks like?
  - Is there anything that got in the way of doing it? Any thoughts or ideas?
  - How did you feel while we did it, and now that you look at what we've done?

Warm-up exercises enable both you and child to familiarise yourself with a spontaneous way of art-making irrespective of technical ability, and to discuss anything upfront that might feel new, different or difficult.

An introduction to using creative art-making to explore and expand upon storybooks

Below we've listed a range of prompts and creative exercises to expand and open further opportunities with children to explore specific themes around storybooks. When children make images, it can be useful to sit with these for a while before rushing into commentary. We think of it as letting an image 'breathe'. Sometimes, practitioners may want to encourage children to look at pictures from different viewpoints. During these moments, the skills of active listening, noticing and gentle observation are essential.

Examples of starter and basic phrases to help explore art images with children

- Let's spend some together looking at this
- I notice, I see, that you've made/put this here
- I wonder what's going on over here?
- I'm going to invite you to ...
- Can you tell me more, can you show me ...?
- This area here, seems different to the rest
- I notice this bit is far away from the rest – I wonder what that's like?
- It's interesting over here ... you've used x, y, z ...
- Let's look at it from this point of view, I wonder what you see
- Let's look at from above, underneath, this corner here
- I wonder about this figure, what they are feeling, what their face might be saying?
- How does this part of your picture feel next to this bit?
- I wonder what might happen if this picture came to life?
- If this part of your picture could speak, or make a sound, what it might be?
- I wonder what kind of conversations might happen between characters/ objects?
- What do you imagine it feels like being this object/creature?
- Any surprises in what you've seen/heard/made?

Chapter 5

Generating immediate creative responses to reading a storybook

- Without speaking, let's draw a response to this storybook
- Let your pen/pencil move freely on the page
  - What shapes, lines, motions, come up?
  - What feelings are evoked?
  - What really stands out from this story?

Exploring characters or elements from the storybooks through art-making

- I wonder if there is a particular moment or a page that attracts you?
  - A character behaving in a way that grabs your attention?
  - If the page were to come to life, what might happen?
- Invite children to make/draw make any response to this page using art materials
  - When finished ... how is your character similar/different?
  - What other things might happen for your character?
- Find a character that is particularly comforting or inspiring (a self-support)
  - How would it be to make your own image of it?
  - What is it about this character that interests you?
  - I wonder what it would be like to include yourself in the picture

Exploring a character's journey

- Let's look at a difficult moment for a character, or a dilemma, a decision-point?
  - Can you show in a picture what they might be finding hard?
  - Make a crossroads map – what do characters have to choose between?
  - Or use speech bubbles to explore how characters make a decision
- What about a moment of positive change in the story, a time of resolution?
  - What led up to this happening?
  - What does it look like?
- Invite children to make their own picture of a story moment that inspires them
  - Exploring different art materials – chalk, pastels, paint, etc
  - Or alternative media – a comic or poster

Using storybooks for creative art-making exercises

Using image making to explore qualities of characters

- In the storybooks, most characters learn and develop new qualities
  - Bravery, kindness, letting go, determination, compassion, etc ...
- What might these qualities feel/look like inside us, our friends, family?
  - Invite children to make a body map to locate these qualities
  - What they might look like, sound like ...
- Invite children to make links to their own selves and bodies
  - Explore which ones they'd like to let go of, or hold on to
  - Experiment with breathing in and breathing out
- Opportunity to explore different faces of a specific quality
  - Determination, kindness, can come in many forms, some unexpected
  - When one might be useful and not useful
  - Putting on a brave face might not always be what's needed – sharing vulnerability can take strength
- Explore with child moments when they have demonstrated specific qualities
  - In life and in room with practitioner
  - Invite child to make an advert, a film poster, of a moment

Looking at what might be going on inside characters – their inner worlds

- Let's look together at what a character in a story might be thinking/feeling
  - Let's go inside and imagine what it feels like from their point of view
  - Invite the child to make speech bubbles to capture thoughts and feelings
  - Encourage children to explore what's going on inside
- When do characters show what they are feeling, when do they hide them
  - Mask-making can be useful here
  - Or design a poster of what we need to help us share our feelings
- I wonder if there are families of feelings – ones that sit more easily together?
  - Which feelings might pull in different or opposite directions?
- Take two opposite feelings for one character, and bring these to life
  - Draw a body map to show where different feelings might live physically
  - Where might characters feel these different emotions inside?
- Explore what the characters in stories do to express feelings
  - Crying, sighing, breathing, curling up, running, jumping up and down
  - Experiment with breathing in and breathing out feelings

Chapter 5

Taking settings from the stories as inspiration and bringing these to life

- Explore some of the natural habitat and settings in the storybooks
  - Island, cave, volcano, forest, seascape, city, village, houses, etc ...
- Can you show me what your own invented house, island, forest, etc looks like?
- Make images from arts materials and use these as a basis for exploration
  - Who/what lives here in your place? People or creatures, anyone?
  - What's it liking living here? Underwater, in a forest, on an island, etc ...?
  - What kind of weather, hot/cold/windy/still – changeable or the same?
- Imagine yourself going into your invented house, cave, underwater world
  - What/who do you see here?
  - How does it feel stepping into this world?
  - What happens here?
- Explore natural metaphors further – volcanos, islands, bridges, trees, cave
  - What might it be like to be an actual bridge, an island, trees, volcano?
  - What changes might they go through?
  - What would happen if they got their own story?

Creating/acting out new dialogue and/or new interactions between characters

- How do the characters get on with each other?
  - How do they speak or treat each other?
- What is left unsaid or undone between characters?
  - What might stop characters from saying things that matter to them?
  - What would you have them say or do?
- What might be too hard or difficult to say, or do?
  - What helps us say/do things that might be difficult?
- Bring to life conversations/interactions between characters as you wish
  - Reading it, performing out loud or enacting it silently
  - Making speech bubbles, or creating own cartoon characters' story
  - Puppets and/or sand tray can also be used here

Creating own characters and story version

- Exploring what doesn't happen in the story but might
- If you were going to draw other versions or endings, what would they look like?
  - If you were going to make a sequel, or prequel ...
- If you were going to make your own book/story what would you do?
- What kind of characters would you follow in their story?
- If you were going to design/make your own helper
  - What would they look like/what would they say/how would they help?
- How would your characters help or support each other?
  - What would they learn?
- Children can design and make their own books with paper
  - Experiment with forms – storyboards, cartoon strips

Taking themes and stories from books and translating these to other creative media

- Can you show me how you would tell or act out this story?
  - 2D – a comic strip, a game, storyboards
  - 3D – through moving miniature toy, sand-play figures, puppets
- What happens in your version? Anything different?
- What do your habitat and surroundings look like?
- What's your beginning, middle and ending?
- What challenges/difficulties do your characters have to deal with?
- Who are the helpers, supporters of the characters?
- How does your story turn out?

Making links with your client's own story through guided creative exercises

- Invite child to lie down on big piece of paper, and draw around them – a body map – to find a home for feelings
  - Can you fill in/decorate your body map – a country, nature, landscape etc?
  - Where do you place your different feelings, thoughts, fears, worries etc?
  - Where are the calm spaces or potential places for calm, positive feelings?

Chapter 5

- Invite child to make a safe place with art materials – could be a place they know or an imaginary place, for example, a den, a tree, a nest, etc
  - What do you want to keep inside your safe place?
  - What would you like to keep outside?
  - How does it feel being inside this safe place?
- Invite child to make a circle of support, or a family and friends' tree of support

Exploring feelings

- Invite a child to blow feelings into a balloon, then let the balloon go
  - How is it to let go of these feelings? And let go of the balloon?
  - What helps us express feelings?
- What shapes do you imagine certain feelings take?
  - Let's look at anger, sadness, guilt, comfort, relief, etc
  - Are some feelings easier than others?
- Encourage children to make images of these in whatever form they like
  - Abstract shapes, forms, textures
  - Cartoon characters
- How might different feelings communicate with each other?

Using Nature's elements as metaphor to explore a child's feelings and conflicts

- If we imagined feelings taking form in elements fire, air, water, earth …
  - I wonder which feeling/s would belong to each element?
  - What might they look/feel/move/sound like?
- Let's explore together how different forms might help or harm
  - Water that can nourish or drown, or ice that freezes
  - Air/wind that blows away fog, but hurricanes can blow away houses
  - Fire that warms or burns/explodes
  - Earth that provides roots for trees, also we can get stuck in the mud
- Let's explore what different elements and energies need to change/transform
  - Giving voice to fears or beliefs to elements around this
  - I wonder how ice feels about melting/what it might need to hear?
- Natural metaphors can be an opportunity to explore polar themes
  - Self-regulation – exploding, releasing, blocking

Using storybooks for creative art-making exercises

- ○ Themes of neglect and lack of care, being cared for, caring for others
- ○ Issues around lack of trust and trust – trusting others, trusting self
- ○ Voicing needs, hiding needs
- ○ Self-protection/protecting others
- It can be useful to also experiment with mood music in background

Using metaphor to explore relationships in a child's world

- Invite children to use metaphors to draw themselves, family members, friends
  - ○ Drawing self and other as different elements or creatures
  - ○ Could be trees, plants, animals (land, underwater, air) superheroes, etc.
  - ○ Explore the places where these characters or creatures might live
- How do the characters in your child's world get on with each other?
  - ○ What kind of conversations happen? How do they talk to each other?
  - ○ Encourage children to invent dialogue between characters
  - ○ What kind of stories happen here?

Creating a fairy tale that links with a child's life

- I wonder if you could create or choose a story about your life
  - ○ What would be the beginning, the middle and end?
  - ○ Who would be the characters, the helpers, what would happen?
  - ○ What would be the decisions, the moments of change in your life?
  - ○ What would you like to change?
  - ○ What would bring your characters peace of mind?

Turning key storybook scenes into guided visualisations and mindfulness exercises

Guided visualisations are a useful way to help ground and calm children while inviting them to connect with their imagination and inner resources. They can also be an introduction to mindfulness exercises. Sometimes, it can be useful to take a favourite scene or familiar character from a storybook as a starting point. It's beneficial to devise and practise these before sessions, so that in the moment you, the practitioner, can present it *live* in the room while attending to the child.

Chapter 5

- The beginning – inviting the child to go inwards on a special journey
  - "I'd like to invite you to take a journey across the sea, mountains, etc"
  - Reaching a safe, special, magical place where you feel warm wind/soft feathers/warm sea/gentle waves, safe nest, tree supporting you, roots, etc
- The middle – you are going to meet a helpful character or magical guide
  - And this guide gives you a gift with magical powers
  - Or whispers something in your ear
  - Or takes you underwater/in the air/on the waves/over hills/through grass
  - Or brings light/calmness/warm flow/different colours into your body
- The end – saying thank you, goodbye to the magical guide and returning to the room
  - Inviting the child to share what they have experienced during this journey

You can use visualisations as one-offs where children are invited to make art-pieces to capture their experience.

- When you're ready, use the materials and bring what you saw to life on the paper
- Any surprises?

Equally, if certain visualisations prove popular, they can become a ritual part of a session without necessarily requiring artwork to be made.

Top tips to remember when working with children and art-making exercises

Chapter 5: Top tips

Top tips for practitioners

Art activities allow children to be free in their expression and to draw inspiration from their own worlds and those they find in storybooks. It's important to allow children space and materials to be experimental and messy, to work alone or in groups, to talk about their work and enjoy the creative process.

If you as a practitioner are not confident with arts materials, focus on a single technique each session – as you become more confident at working with materials creatively combine techniques in sessions as you wish. You don't have to be an artist to deliver a creative activity – the first step is to have an open mind, focus on the process and not the outcome, choose a technique you are comfortable working with and enjoy the experience:

1. Painting
2. Drawing & colouring
3. Collage
4. Sand play
5. Model making
6. Print making

There are no rules in art – but it is important to be organised as a practitioner working with creative approaches.

- Make the sure the space you have is suitable for the activity
- Think about how long the activity will take – give it space
- Make sure you have enough materials for the activity you have planned
- Choosing whether your activity is 'wet' or 'dry' is important
- If you are working with 'wet' materials like paints or inks, make sure you have thought about
  - Table or floor coverings
  - Aprons
  - A water supply nearby for cleaning your equipment
  - Plastic gloves and wet wipes (some children don't like to be messy)
  - Space for your 'wet' artwork to dry – and drying time

This list also applies to collage – gluing and sticking, sand play and model making.

A large part of working with creative activities is practical, setting up and clearing up. It's also important to teach children to respect their materials and look after them properly. Packing up carefully and cleaning brushes etc is also a valuable part of the process. If you give enough time and don't rush, children can appreciate the importance of clearing away.

Once you are set up – try to relax – let the creative process lead and see what happens. It helps not to have a preconceived idea of what to expect from an outcome – children will always surprise you!

EXAMPLE WORKSHEETS
Worksheets for process-orientated warm-up creative activities

Chapter 5: Example worksheets

Worksheet for process-orientated warm-up creative activities

STARTER WARM-UP – BREATHING COLOUR

Aim: To help children get in touch with free play and give permission for creative art-making, equally to get in touch with sensory feelings

Examples of creative materials: To be scaled up and down in accordance with resources

Arts materials: Paper, card, pens, crayons

STEPS and INSTRUCTIONS

Bringing our breath to life through colour
- We are going to make an image of our breathing on the paper with different colours

Start to notice your breath
- Notice how it comes into and out of your body
- You might want to blow onto your hand both slowly or quickly, or suck in your breath

I'm going to invite you to make/draw an image or patterns on the paper of how you breathe
- Imagine your breath as dancing and coming out onto the page
- Pick up a colour crayon and make a line or shape that follows your breath
- You can slow down or speed up with your breath and your drawing
- If you like, experiment with different colours on your page

When you're ready, stop and let's sit with the image in silence
- Without speaking, notice what shapes, patterns, colours you've used
- Notice what the different kinds of breath look like on a page
- Before we talk about it, is there anything you feel like you want to add?

Reflections on the BREATHING COLOUR exercise
- What's it like to experiment with different breathing? Fast, slow, holding breath?
- What do you notice about the image you've made?
- What does your image make you think of, feel?

Worksheet for process-orientated warm-up creative activities

STARTER WARM-UP – DECORATING HAND DRAWINGS

Aim: To help children get in touch with free play and give permission for creative art-making, equally to explore what they use their hands for, their creative power

Examples of creative materials: To be scaled up and down in accordance with resources

Arts materials: Paper, card, pens, crayons, pastels, glitter, ribbons, fabric, buttons, etc

STEPS and INSTRUCTIONS

Getting to know our hands
- Let's spend a moment looking at your hands, feeling, touching them

I'm going to invite you to make an image of your hands by drawing around them
- Think about what you use them for, what things you like to do with your hands
- Draw around your hands on one piece of paper
- You can place or position them in any way you like, use any colours you like

Decorate your hands
- In whatever way you'd like, take some time to decorate the hands you've made
- It may be inside your hands or outside your hands, whatever you'd like

When you're ready, stop and let's sit with your drawn hands for a moment in silence
- Without speaking, notice what shapes, patterns, colours you've used

Reflections on the HAND DRAWINGS exercise
- What do you notice about your hand?
- What's inside the hands outline, what's outside?
- What kind of things do you like doing with your hands?

Chapter 5: Example worksheets

Worksheet for process-orientated warm-up creative activities

STARTER WARM-UP – SCRIBBLE GAME

Aim: To help children get in touch with free play and to remove the fear of being faced with a blank piece of paper

Examples of creative materials: To be scaled up and down in accordance with resources

Arts materials: Paper, card, pens, crayons

STEPS and INSTRUCTIONS

Co-creating a world of scribbles on the page; child and practitioner
- Together with your child client, take a blank piece of paper each
- Choose a colour pen and each of you start to make your own scribble
- Remember you are just scribbling, not making an image
- Try not to lift the pen up from the paper and let your pen take your hand for a walk
- You can close your eyes if you want

Swap your scribble drawing with each other and look to see what shapes you can find – could be landscapes, objects, buildings, creatures and characters – anything!
- Don't try too hard to see things … just see what jumps out
- Pick up a different colour pen/s and draw what you see inside/around the shapes
- Remember there is no right or wrong, and you may want to add words too

Share your images together
- Repeat the exercise again, either on the same paper, or using a bigger piece
- Share your scribble drawings, and present your objects/characters to each other
  - You may want to give them made-up names or titles

This time, after you've finished, choose a few characters or objects from your scribble drawing and make up a quick story about them
- Don't worry about the story making sense … just start with *Once Upon a Time …*

Reflections on the *SCRIBBLE GAME* exercise

- How was it to scribble freely on the paper like this?
- What was it like to find all these different things inside the scribbles?
- Any surprises about the scribble game, or anything you've learnt about yourself?

EXAMPLE WORKSHEETS
Worksheets for process-orientated creative art-making activities

Chapter 5: Example worksheets

Worksheet for process-orientated creative art-making activities

WHAT'S MISSING FROM THE PICTURE?

Choose an image from a storybook and imagine what else could be included

Aim: To support children with their engagement and understanding of the story

Examples of creative materials: To be scaled up and down in accordance with resources

Arts materials: Paper, pencil, card, pens, paint, chalk pastels

STEPS and INSTRUCTIONS

Choose a picture from a storybook
- We are going to use our imaginations to explore the images in this storybook and see what isn't in the picture, and what else could be added
- Let's look in depth at this storybook, and select one picture that grabs your attention
  - What is it about this image that really attracts you?
  - Colours, shapes, activity of interest?

Imagine what else could be happening in this scene
- What or who might be hidden from view?
  - What's happening off the page or around the corner?
  - What do you imagine might happen next instead?

Draw or paint a picture of what else you see happening
- Feel free to use your imagination
  - Add anything that you'd like to be part of this story
  - What colours would you use to create your scene?

Retelling the story
- Share your new picture, making up a new story about what's going on inside it

78

Worksheet for process-orientated creative art-making activities

MASK MAKING AND ROLE-PLAY

Aim: To invite children to engage with characters and supportive dialogue in a story

Examples of creative materials: To be scaled up and down in accordance with resources

Natural materials: Shells, sand, leaves

Arts materials: Cardboard, paper, pencil, pens, paint, chalk pastels, ribbons, fabrics, glitter, sticky jewels, glue, tissue paper, paint, cotton wool, wool, tinfoil, plastic masks

STEPS and INSTRUCTIONS

Choose a character, creature or object that you would like to know more about in this book
- You are going to make a mask of this character/creature/object so we can start to have a conversation with them
  - Take your time making your mask to bring your chosen character to life
  - Feel free to play with the materials
  - It may become something else during the making
  - You might want to give it your own name

Become this character
- Spend some time being this character, putting on the mask
  - How do they talk and/or sound, do they sound like someone you know?
  - What do they have to say?
  - What does it feel like being this character?

Have a dialogue with this character
- Invite someone to put on the mask and have a conversation with your character
  - Any questions you would like to ask it?
  - What is going on for your character?

Retell/re-enact the story
- Can you create a new story for the character mask you've made?

79

Chapter 5: Example worksheets

Worksheet for process-orientated creative art-making activities

CREATE YOUR FAVOURITE STORY SCENE (3D)

Aim: To support children in creating a magical place to visit

Examples of creative materials: To be scaled up and down in accordance with resources

Recycled materials: A shoebox, other boxes, fabrics, whatever is at hand

Natural materials: Shells, sand, leaves, twigs, feathers, straw

Arts materials: Paper, card, pens, glitter, sticky jewels, glue, tissue paper, paint, cotton wool, plasticine, cocktail sticks, masking tape, cellophane, bubble wrap, crinkly card, string

STEPS and INSTRUCTIONS

Initial considerations
- Choose a storybook and read it through carefully looking at the pictures, which scene tempts you – which scene makes you feel as if you would like to be there?
- Look at the materials you have available and choose materials that remind you of that scene – think about the colours/textures/shapes
- Use an empty shoebox or any similar sized box and begin to create your scene

Methods & ideas
- Paint or colour the inside of the box to resemble the place in the story
- Add materials to painted background, e.g. cotton wool to make clouds in a sky
- Create ground effect by adding leaves/grass/sand to floor of the box
- Hang things from the ceiling of the box for a 3D effect – were there birds flying in the sky that day?
- Make and add other parts of the scene; buildings, animals, trees or rocks – (even simply drawing onto card and then folding the base to attach to base of the box works well)

Process-orientated creative art-making activities

Retell the story
- When your box is complete imagine yourself in the place you have created. How do you feel?
- Introduce someone to your world and tell them why it is a special place
- Keep your box as somewhere you can visit whenever you want to

Chapter 5: Example worksheets

Worksheet for process-orientated creative art-making activities

WORKING WTH THE SENSORY LANDSCAPE FROM A CHOSEN STORYBOOK

Aim: To support children to deepen their engagement with the story

Examples of creative materials: To be scaled up and down in accordance with resources

Arts materials: Paper, pencil, card, pens, paint, chalk pastels, collage materials, leaves, found objects with different textures i.e. bubble wrap. Use music or recordings of nature sounds as appropriate (bird song/sea sounds)

STEPS and INSTRUCTIONS

Choose a picture from a storybook
- Look through the storybook and observe the colours that have been used
- Look at the type of trees/animals/terrain that feature in the story
- What part of the world do you think it was set in? A hot climate or a cold climate? A particular country that you might know about?

Imagine how you would feel if you were there? Close your eyes and imagine (you can also play a sound tape to help the child enter the world of the story)

- Would you be hot or cold?
  - What sounds would you be hearing?
  - What smells would you be smelling?
  - What textures would you be feeling?

Draw/paint or collage a response to what else you have imagined

- Use warm OR cold colours to create the background
- Add anything else that you'd like to be part of this picture

Retell the story

- Share your new art piece
- Talk about the sensory details you imagined – touch/smell/sight/sound

Chapter 5: Example worksheets

Worksheet for process-orientated creative art-making activities

MEMORY BOXES

Aim: To support children in gathering stories and memories about loved ones, and keeping them in a special place

Examples of creative materials: To be scaled up and down in accordance with resources

Recycled materials: A shoe box, other boxes, ribbons, fabrics, whatever is at hand

Natural materials: Shells, sand, leaves

Arts materials: Paper, card, pens, glitter, sticky jewels, glue, tissue paper, paint, cotton wool

STEPS and INSTRUCTIONS

- We are going to make a memory box today to put special memories inside of a loved one, decorating the outside and inside of a box

Ideas for the OUTSIDE of the box
- Spend some time thinking about the person you are wanting to remember
  - What stories do you remember about this person?
  - What has this person loved doing during their life?
  - What colour/s, an animal, flowers/trees, make you think of this person?
- Decorate the outside of the box in any way you'd like to remember this person
  - You may want to draw/paint pictures or shapes on the outside of the box
  - Or write special words, names
- Think about if you'd like a special closure on this box
  - A ribbon, stickers

Ideas for the INSIDE of the box
- How would you like to decorate the inside of this box to make it feel special and safe?
  - You might want to think about a nest, or a special space or place
- Tissue paper, or cotton wool, or fabric can help create a "landing place"
- What do you want to remember about this person?

- Write down or draw memories of you and them together
- Thoughts, poems, songs
- Any messages that you'd like to store here for this loved one?
- Any objects or photos that you'd like to place here?

Create a special 'ritual' ending for the MEMORY BOX

- Think about where to keep your box and who you'd like to show it to
- You can keep on adding anything you'd like inside and outside the box
- You may want to take it out on special anniversaries

Summary and conclusions

We hope that this Storybook Manual provides a practical source of ideas when supporting children going through loss and difficult life transitions. In providing a wide range of therapeutic and creative interventions, practitioners can pick and choose depending on what works for them and their clients. It is also our hope that practitioners will be inspired to develop their own ideas working in their field and context, including parents and caregivers where they can.

One of the unique gifts of children's storybooks is their dual presentation of words and pictures, enabling the non-verbal and verbal to live side by side. We believe that this enables right and left-brain activity to happen naturally as children make their own links through the medium of metaphor.

Sometimes it's not the right time for words. Maybe it's too early and time may need to pass before raw feeling can find form in words. Or maybe, we are working with children in extreme situations where words just don't translate the depth and intensity of emotions being evoked. In these moments, storybook pictures can really help. A metaphor can sum up what words might struggle to capture. Image and metaphor speak to our imagination, and the deepest parts of ourselves. That is why the Storybook Manual encourages the need for pacing when working with images without rushing into commentary. At other times, a storybook's phrase can be a starting point to find words for feelings. Being able to reflect verbally can be enormously helpful, as children try to process what is going on inside them, around them.

Education in schools has its natural focus on literacy, in teaching children to read and write. We would like to reiterate the visual literacy that most children naturally have, and often don't need to be taught. We hope that by taking away from art some of the pressure around skill and technique, that image-making can empower children

Summary and conclusions

to share real feelings and life stories in creative ways. Although life inevitably brings change and hardship to us all, some children have difficult childhoods that leave them with fewer inner resources. If we can give children the space and time to engage with their emotional landscapes, validating their experience, helping them make sense of it, then hopefully they learn invaluable skills – a capacity for resilience, flexibility, listening, curiosity, self-expression, self-knowledge, relationship, creativity – that stand them in good stead for meeting the challenges of the future.

Finally, one core premise of our work is shared learning and practice. We would love to hear how practitioners find their own ways to use storybooks creatively and therapeutically in their specific fields. For ideas that you've developed that you are willing to share, or ideas that you've found particularly beneficial from this Storybook Manual, please do drop us a line.

Many thanks,
Pia and Sarah

Bibliography

AXLINE, V (1947)   *Play Therapy*, Boston, MA: Houghton Mifflin

BALINT, M (1968/1989)   *The Basic Fault: Therapeutic Aspects of Regression*, London: Routledge

BETTLEHEIM, B (1976)   *The Uses of Enchantment*, London: Penguin

BOWLBY, J (1988)   *A Secure Base*, London: Routledge

BRETT, D (1988)   *Annie Stories: A Special Kind of Storytelling*, New York, NY: Workman Publishing

BULMER, L (2000)   *Using Picture Books in Drama Therapy with Children: A Therapeutic Model*, MA Research Paper, Concordia University, Montreal

CAMPBELL, J (1993)   *The Hero with a Thousand Faces*, London: Fontana Press

CASEMENT, P (1985)   *On Learning from the Patient*, London: Routledge

CATTANACH, A (1994)   *Play Therapy: Where the Sky Meets the Underworld*, London: Jessica Kingsley Press

GELDARD, D & GELDARD, K (1997)   *Counselling Children: A Practical Introduction*, London: Sage

GREENALGH, P (1997)   *Emotional Growth & Learning*, London: Routledge

HOLMES, J (1993)   *John Bowlby & Attachment Theory*, London: Routledge

HUGHES, D (2007)   *Attachment: Focused Family Therapy*, New York, NY: WW Norton

JENNINGS, S (1998)   *Introduction to Dramatherapy*, London: Jessica Kingsley

JENNINGS, S (2005)   *Creative Play & Drama with Adults at Risk*, Bicester: Speechmark Publishing

Bibliography

JONES, P (1996)	*Drama as Therapy: Theatre as Living*, London: Jessica Kingsley Press
JUNG, CG (1964)	*Man and His Symbols*, London: Picador
JUNG, CG (1984)	*The Spirit in Man, Art & Literature*, London: Ark
LEVINE, S (1992)	*Poesis*, London: Jessica Kingsley
MCNIFF, S (1992)	*Art as Medicine, Creating a Therapy of the Imagination*, London: Piatkus
MILLS, JC & CROWLEY, RJ (1986)	*Therapeutic Metaphors for Children and the Child Within*, New York, NY: Brunner/Mazel
OAKLANDER, V (1988)	*Windows to our Children*, Gouldsboro ME: Gestalt Journal Press
OUP (2005)	*Oxford Dictionary of Phrase and Fable*, Oxford: Oxford University Press
ROGERS, C (1980)	*A Way of Being*, Boston, MA: Houghton Mifflin
SIEGELMAN, E (1990)	*Metaphor and Meaning in Psychotherapy*, New York, NY: Guilford Press
SPITZ, E (1999)	*Inside Picture Books*, New Haven, CT: Yale University Press
STERN, DN (1985)	*The Interpersonal World of the Infant*, New York, NY: Basic Books
WHITTICK, A (1960)	*Symbols, Signs and Their Meaning*, London: Leonard Hill
WINNICOTT, D (1947)	"Hate in the Counter-Transference", based on a paper read to the British Psycho-Analytical Society, 5 February 1947, originally published in *The International Journal of Psycho-Analysis* (1949; 30: 69–74).
WINNICOTT, D (1964)	*The Child, the Family & the Outside World*, London: Penguin
WINNICOTT, D (1971)	*Playing and Reality*, London: Tavistock

Permissions

"More often than not, he (the child) is unable to express these feelings in words, or he can do so only by indirection: fear of the dark, of some animal, anxiety about his body. The fairy tale takes these existential anxieties and dilemmas very seriously and addresses itself directly to them: the need to be loved and the fear that one is thought worthless; the love of life and the fear of death." (Bettleheim, 1976: 10).

From *The Uses of Enchantment: The Meaning and Importance of Fairy Tales* by Bruno Bettelheim, © 1975, 1976 by Bruno Bettelheim. Reprinted by kind permission of Thames & Hudson, Ltd., London.